THE EMPLOYEE ENGAGEMENT HANDBOOK

LUCA DELLANNA

Luca Dellanna

@DellAnnaLuca
Luca-dellanna.com

First edition
March 2024 update
Luca Dell'Anna © 2024 – All Rights Reserved

CONTENTS

Introduction   v

PART I
MEETING THE FIVE EMPLOYEE NEEDS

1. Need #1: Compensation   3
2. Need #2: Growth   7
3. Need #3: Impact and recognition   23
4. Need #4: Being treated as an individual   30
5. Need #5: Removing toil   34
6. Summary of Part I   43

PART II
CREATING CHANGE

7. Rolling out change   51
8. Create change within your team   54
9. Involve other managers in the change initiative   56
10. Create local change   58
11. Deploying change within the whole organization   61

Conclusions   64

About the Author   67
Also by Luca Dellanna   69
Winning Long-Term Games   70
Ergodicity   72
Best Practices for Operational Excellence   73
The Control Heuristic   74
Managing Hybrid and Remote Teams   75
100 Truths   76
The World Through a Magnifying Glass   77
Acknowledgments   79

INTRODUCTION

I have worked on talent retention for more than 13 years, both as a manager, leading groups of up to 40 people, and as a consultant, having worked with tens of corporations worldwide and hundreds of managers.

My experience led me to the following observations:

1) **Retaining employees is important, but the real goal is to retain engagement.** What you really want to avoid is employees giving up being *active and engaged* members of your organization.

2) **Employees give up when they no longer believe that being active members of the organization is worth the time and effort.** Indifference is a symptom of having forgotten that good outcomes follow good work.

3) **Once an employee gives up, it's hard to remotivate them.** Hence, you must address sources of frustration *before* they cause people to give up.

4) **Money is everything and nothing.** It's everything because if you don't compensate your people fairly, they will give up. And it's

Introduction

nothing because even if you pay above-market rates, they will still give up if they don't grow, feel valued, or their work environment is too frustrating.

5) Managers and supervisors have extreme leverage on employee retention, for good and for bad. Hence, they should be the primary touchpoint of any initiative to reduce turnover and increase engagement.

Before continuing, let me give you a few examples of what I mean by "employees give up when they undergo experiences that teach them that being an active and engaged member of the organization is not worth the time and effort."

Experiences teaching it's NOT worth being engaged	Experiences teaching it's worth being engaged
Working hard without it being acknowledged or it leading to some form of growth	One's good work being acknowledged or leading to some form of growth
Having to do extra work because of someone else's mistake (including unclear delegation or poor planning)	Seeing the impact of one's work (e.g., interacting with final users, seeing a product launch, receiving a genuine acknowledgement from a colleague)
Having to regularly perform tasks that are more tiring than they should because of a lack of adequate resources or because of a lack of care from the people having designed them	Having adequate resources that allow one to focus on the substance of their work. Toil is reduced to the reasonable minimum
Having one's time wasted	Having one's time respected and being treated like a valuable professional
Being withhold information	Receiving full context and generally being trusted with information and access above the minimum required
Being told an idea is bad or cannot be implemented without being explained why	Ideas are listened and either implemented or rejected for good reason, which is well explained and understood
Bringing up problems and nothing ever changing	Problems are addressed (or a good reason why not is explained)

Introduction

As we will see later in the handbook, an important part of an effective employee retention strategy involves minimizing the events in the left column and substituting them with those in the right column.

The employees' point of view

Over the past eleven years, I've conducted tens of consulting engagements that included interviewing employees. Here are their five most common needs, in no particular order.

Need	Examples
I want to earn a fair living	– I want to earn enough to satisfy my living standards – If I go above and beyond, I want to be compensated for it – I don't want others in the same role as me to earn more with no good reason
I want growth (and be helped to grow)	– I want my job and salary to evolve over time – I want to be supported in my growth *(i.e., the opportunities need not only to be there but I should be reasonably helped achieve them, e.g., through coaching and/or clear and actionable objectives for the next step)*
I want impact and recognition	– I want my manager to acknowledge the difficulties of my job – I want my manager to acknowledge when I do a good job – I want to see the impact I make with my work on its *direct* beneficiaries (customers, users, or colleagues)
I want to be treated as an individual	– I want my manager and colleagues to know a few things about me – I want my job to be adapted to my strength and weaknesses, within reason
I don't want toil	– I don't want my tasks to be unnecessarily tedious or tiring – I don't want to have to do extra work because of others' incompetence or lack of care

Introduction

In the following chapters, I will go through each of these needs and provide a few concrete systems in which organizations can meet them.

Handbook overview

In **Part I: The Five Needs**, I will talk to you as if you were a manager and guide you on how to fulfill the needs of your team to improve their engagement and retention.

In **Part II: Creating Change**, I will talk to you as if you were a business leader and will guide you into implementing the principles of Part I at the scale of the organization.

Any questions?

Feel free to email me at **Luca@Luca-Dellanna.com**; I read all emails personally and usually reply within 48 hours.

Share your learnings!

It's okay, encouraged even, to share quotes or screenshots of a few paragraphs from this book on social media! Just remember to mention the author and title. You can even share the whole PDF with your colleagues.

Conversely, adapting the contents, reselling them, or sharing without attribution is not okay.

Disclaimer

Always use common sense. Nothing in this book is financial advice or advice of any other kind. The author shall not be held liable for the application or misapplication of the contents of this book. You can find a link to my full disclaimer at **Luca-dellanna.com**

PART I

MEETING THE FIVE EMPLOYEE NEEDS

In the first part of this handbook, I will cover the concrete actions you can take to meet the five needs of the employees in your team:

1. Compensation.
2. Growth.
3. Impact and recognition.
4. Being treated as individuals.
5. As little toil and frustration as possible.

1

NEED #1: COMPENSATION

Obviously, your employees want to be paid for their work. Not only that, but they also want to be compensated fairly:

– They want to be paid market wages. If your company cannot afford to pay market wages for your local market, it probably means its productivity is below average.

In this case, you have two solutions: (1) employ or outsource in cheaper markets, and (2) increase your productivity.

The latter is an under-discussed option – to be more precise, it is discussed at the higher levels of the organization (hopefully), but it is often *not* discussed at lower levels, or at least not nearly enough.

In the next chapter ("Need #2: growth"), I explain how not only should your company offer top-down growth options such as career paths but also individually stimulate its employees to grow their skills and productivity so that they can be paid higher wages.

– If your people go above and beyond and produce increased revenue or lower costs for your organization, they expect to get a piece of it. For example, a line worker who comes up with an idea that ends up saving tens of thousands of dollars a year in manufacturing costs expects to receive a sizeable bonus (or a raise).

This means two things. First, obviously, you should reward those who help your company make more profits, and that reward should be enough to make them feel like they've been treated fairly.

And second, you should look out for workers who go above and beyond in ways you cannot reward and redirect their efforts toward more productive venues, or at least have a frank conversation to prevent them from being disappointed by expecting a reward that cannot (and shouldn't) come.

– Your employees will feel betrayed if a colleague with a similar role and contribution makes more than them.

To prevent this, you should do three things.

First, have consistent pay levels and job ladders across your whole organization.

Second, if an employee is given a higher salary than their colleagues because they bring more value or are expected to bring more value, that should be explained clearly and in a way that promises the following: "If you also do it, you will also get the raise."

Third, you should always explain what would warrant higher salaries or bonuses *before you get asked about it*. Failure to do so would mean missing a great opportunity to stimulate growth and increase perceived fairness.

Before explaining how to concretely practice this last point, here are a few more words on fairness. It is possible to pay your workers fairly, yet them believe they're paid unfairly.

This was my case in my former corporate job, when I thought my full-time employee hourly salary was unfairly low as compared to freelance consultants' hourly rate – without realizing that their billable hours are a small part of their month and that they have to pay for their own taxes, between other downsides of freelancing.

The lesson is to not only strive to offer a fair salary but also explain why it's fair, and not with abstract corporate-speak but with concrete details.

Some examples below:

– "We pay you a fraction of what we bill our clients for your time because our client rates must also cover unbillable work and other overhead such as sales and project coordination, plus they pay for flexibility."

– "We don't pay as much as a San Francisco company because the costs of living here are much lower, and you actually end up with a higher disposable outcome."

The more talented your people are, the more you should discuss whether they believe their salary to be fair *before it seems necessary to do so.* I've seen too many companies lose talent because, one day, they start asking themselves if they are underpaid and consequently explore other job options. At this point, even if you manage to convince them to stay, they won't be as dedicated as they were previously.

Compensation growth

Especially with middle management and below, many compensation issues are productivity issues. "Do I get enough value out of this worker to afford paying them a high wage? And do I get enough marginal growth out of paying my workers more to justify investing in higher wages instead of other investment opportunities?"

While there are obvious productivity bounds placed by industry- and local considerations, in most companies, **there are huge margins of growth in how much individuals can be helped to become more productive, thus justifying the higher wages that will keep them more engaged.**

The next chapter discusses how to achieve these gains.

Further readings

Claire Hughes Johnson's book *"Scaling People"* excellently describes how to set up consistent hiring, growth, and compensation systems.

2

NEED #2: GROWTH

Your people want personal growth, which, depending on the individual aptitude, might mean a different mix of salary growth, responsibility growth, autonomy growth, skills growth, and prestige growth.

Crucially, **almost all your employees want growth, even those who don't seem to take any action towards it.**

It's a bit like romantic partners: some say they are looking for one, and many don't take much action towards that, but that doesn't mean that most without a partner don't feel lonely. Often, the reason one doesn't take action isn't a lack of desire but a lack of know-how or lack of opportunity.

It is your job to provide everyone with the know-how and opportunity needed to grow – *even those who don't demand it.*

First of all, because most people who don't grow end up disengaged and demotivated – even if they didn't ask for growth. And second, because the desire for growth is often downstream, not upstream, skills and actionable opportunities.

I've seen this over and over in my career: someone deemed disengaged regaining engagement after being given a way to grow. Here is the bottleneck, though: **the less engaged the person, the more specific and actionable the step forward must be** for it to be taken action against.

If a person is disengaged, just mentioning a career path or specialization to them won't be enough. They won't take it unless the path toward it is clear and feels actionable. Moreover, they must trust that they have a real chance at it as opposed to risking wasting their efforts.

Of course, in an ideal world, people would either take ownership of their growth or not complain about the lack thereof. However, this is not an ideal world, and most of the workforce expects growth to happen to them and will be disappointed otherwise. It's not that they don't want to do their part; it's that they want to be told very specifically what they have to do for them to grow, and they want to see progress, not promises.

Therefore, you have two options.

Option #1, only hire A+ candidates who fully and proactively take their growth into their hands.

Option #2, take responsibility for the development of your people and give them individual objectives for personal growth that are specific and actionable enough so that most of your workers will take action against them. Anything else is bound to lead to a mostly disengaged workforce that will add tons of friction to your operations.

The first option is hard, especially at scale, but if you think you can pull it off, by all means, go for it. Otherwise, the next few pages will help you implement the second one.

Taking charge of your people's growth

The table below compares two growth paradigms.

Personal growth is pulled	Personal growth is pushed
"Career paths" detail vertical growth options and are available on demand	"Career paths" detail vertical, horizontal, and within-position growth options, and are proactively discussed by managers with all their subordinates
Managers support their subordinates to meet their role's expectations, but growth beyond that is left to the subordinate's personal initiative	Managers support their subordinates to meet their role's expectations and to grow beyond that
Skills are taught during onboarding, when minimum standards aren't met, or upon individiual request	Managers constantly teach their subordinates how to get better at their work or set actionable objectives that specifically encourage them to acquire new skills or improve existing ones
Managers delegate tasks and objectives based on "what needs to get done"	Managers delegate tasks and objectives not just based on "what needs to get done" but also "what could increase the report's skills / responsibility / impact / trust / proactiveness

As you can see, moving from the first to the second paradigm mostly requires managers to take responsibility for their subordinate's growth and for the growth of their contribution beyond meeting standards.

First, let's see what this means concretely, and then let's discuss how you can get your managers to adopt such behaviors.

Career paths

Your company should have career paths: answers to questions such as "You got hired as a junior developer; here is what career growth in this company could look like for you." Such career paths should be well documented and freely available upon request. This is table stakes.

That said, **traditional career paths alone aren't sufficient to satisfy your people's development needs. One reason is that in most companies, there isn't room for everyone to grow vertically. Therefore, you should also have horizontal and within-position growth options.** Examples of the latter are growth across levels (e.g., junior → mid-level → senior) or specializations (e.g., expertise in a specific tool or customer type, becoming a mentor, getting into an internal working group, eventually leading it, etc.) The specifics vary depending on the role at hand, but the principle is the same: everyone should have options for growth.

Moreover, you should proactively discuss these options with your people, for example, during one-on-ones, and invite them to pick one – not as a definitive choice, but as something to work towards.

Of course, you should guide and inform their choice as necessary to ensure they choose realistic objectives. You don't want to promise growth that cannot happen, nor do you want everyone to chase the same position. Instead, you want to realistically advise and inform your people and provide options that work for everyone.

Some concrete examples of career paths

For a sales assistant / retail clerk:

– Vertical options: store manager → area manager → country manager, trainer → trainer of trainers, etc.

– Horizontal options: move to a different (larger?) store, etc.

– Within-position options *(additional roles on top of the current position)*: mentor, social media influencer, internal training content producer, etc.

For a management consultant:

– Vertical options: junior → mid-level → senior, consultant → project leader → engagement manager, etc.

– Horizontal options: move to different office locations, to teams working on different industries, etc.

– Within-position options: specialize in a particular kind of project or problem, master a particular tool or software, etc.

Should the within-position options be coupled with a raise? A modest one would be fair, enticing, and would force you to provide options that provide real value and to train the people in them so that they provide as much value as possible. That said, even unpaid growth options are better than no option at all.

Talking about career paths and growth options

When discussing career paths and growth options, it's important that you provide a full picture. What does this new role do concretely? If you want to get there, what does the path look like, concretely? What will you have to do, and to what standard? What's the next step toward it?

In the case of a vertical or horizontal option, you should mention whether openings are limited and explain the selection criteria. You should be realistic and specific about what you think the chances of success are, but if your subordinate commits to it, you should do your best to set them up for success.

As long as you've been sincere and realistic, provided accurate feedback, and have been helpful, your subordinate's trust and loyalty in you will increase even if they don't get the position – whereas if you over-promise or fail to support your subordinate, they will lose trust in you and perhaps in the organization.

Conflicts of interest

Some managers are reticent to push their subordinates to grow because they believe it would make them more demanding and lead to them quitting. I disagree: lack of growth is a much larger risk.

Others don't want their subordinates to grow because they need them in their current position. Then, just offer within-position opportunities!

Stimulate everyone's growth

Managers should stimulate everyone[1]'s growth, not just towards career paths but also at a more granular level, providing developmental steps that feel actionable.

The idea is that the manager and the subordinate agree on a *specific and actionable* short-term development goal during their weekly one-on-one; then, the subordinate works on it while the manager reviews progress and does what's needed to set them up for success.

Easier said than done, obviously, so let's see how to do it properly.

The most common mistake is to set development goals that are too big and generic, such as "learn this tool" or "contribute to a deal." Because they are too big and generic, they are often met with inaction or procrastination ("Where do I even start?" "Can I really do it?" "Where do I find the time?").

Instead, **set development goals that take at most a few hours to complete.** You will find a few examples in the table below.

Objective category	Examples
A specific skill	– Learn pivot tables in Excel – Improve your slide design skills – Learn the internal fire safety audit procedure
A specific action or deliverable	– Analyze the latest sales data for insights on customer behavior – Prepare an internal presentation on the new travel expenses procedure – Follow John during his next internal audit
BEST: a specific action or deliverable realized through a specific skills	– Learn pivot tables in Excel and use them to analyze the latest sales data – Prepare an internal presentation on the new travel expenses procedure, focusing on clear slide design – Read the internal fire safety audit procedure and follow John during his next audit

Development goals are distinct from long-term growth objectives.

The latter are taken care of by career paths. Instead, **development goals are steps forward designed to create momentum.**

Their top feature is actionability: the subordinate shouldn't wonder what they should do next, whether they can do it, or whether they have the time.

Development goals should take at most a few hours of work to fulfill (distributed over a month at most). Anything longer is too big and generic and will be forgotten or indefinitely procrastinated.

Ideally, everyone should have a development goal to work on. Then, at some point during the weekly one-on-ones, managers should ask their subordinates whether they made any progress towards their development goal, providing feedback or support as needed. If the development goal is completed, a new one can be agreed upon. Otherwise, the manager should ask the subordinate what they plan to do toward their development goal during the next few days. If the subordinate is particularly busy and their goal requires significant time, it's okay if they say, "I'm too busy this week," – though, if this happens too often, the manager should reduce the scope and choose a smaller goal that can feel more actionable.

Development goals aren't set in stone as KPIs or yearly objectives are. Their objective is to stimulate growth and momentum, so they can be renegotiated until they fulfill their role: being taken action upon and creating growth and momentum.

…

A quick tip: if you have trouble finding development goals for your subordinates, consider the following prompts:

- *Is there any small value-adding task they can learn?*
- *Is there anything that is holding them back?*
- *Is there anything that, if they learned how to do better, would make their job easier?*

The importance of consistency

The most important factor for the success of development goals is whether the manager mentions them during *each* one-on-one. The first time the manager fails to mention them, the subordinate learns the lesson that they are not important and/or the manager doesn't believe in them.

Of course, employees are very busy, and it's okay not to make progress on one's development goal for a week or two. What matters, though, is not to lose momentum, for that would become fertile soil for disengagement.

To prevent that, you should be forgiving of one or two weeks in which your subordinate doesn't work on their development goal, but starting with the third week, you should become gradually more insistent on progress. That said, if progress doesn't come, the reaction should not be to demand performance (as a manager would do in case of lack of progress towards a project or KPI) but instead to renegotiate the development goal towards something that feels more accessible.

…

The best way to support your subordinates in the choice and achievement of their development goals is *coaching* – the object of the following pages.

Coaching

First of all, forget everything you know about coaching, for the term is used for anything and nothing.

For me, to coach someone means to *guide* them into doing what they need to do to become more effective at what they do, and it consists of a mix of:

– **Providing feedback and identifying opportunities for growth.** The more specific, the better *(for example, instead of "You should work on your presentation skills, say, "You should improve your diction and, in particular, get rid of the hmmm sounds").*

– **Teaching** how to do something well. *This includes teaching what it means to do a particular task well and explaining not just what separates good from bad but also good from great.*

– **Roleplaying and playing hypotheticals** to pre-empt mistakes and validate readiness, resulting in fast learning and setting the coachee up for success.

– **Setting long- *and* short-term objectives.** A coachee should end the session with a better and clearer to-do list than when they began it.

– **Creating momentum** by splitting large tasks and projects into more actionable chunks.

– **Providing accountability** by demanding and reviewing progress.

Teaching during coaching

Here are some teaching frameworks I use when coaching.

– **Bad, good, great.** Given a task, role, or objective of the coachee, I explain what a bad performer would do or care about, what a good one would do or care about, and what a great one would do or care about.

– **What's too little, what's too much, and common mistakes.** This is a great framework for delegating tasks and objectives. Explain what a successfully completed task would look like, then mention what would be too little, then what would be too much, and finally, the common mistakes of people working on that task.

– **Roleplay and hypotheticals.** There's nothing better than asking the coachee what they would do in a situation and providing them with some immediate feedback. It allows them to practice in a safe space and discover possible mistakes or misunderstandings without having to go through the effort and pain required by failing in the real world.

A common mistake managers make while coaching is feeling like it's not their place to teach. Maybe they don't feel confident. Or perhaps they don't want to look like micromanagers. But consider that even Cristiano Ronaldo and Michael Jordan had coaches who told them how to play – even if the coaches were clearly worse players than those superstars. That's because even the most talented people need someone to tell them what they cannot see and help them understand how they can improve.

Teach good judgment

Hypotheticals are a great tool for teaching good judgment. Ask your people what they would do in a situation, listen to their answer, and then explain what you think of their decision and why. If you play a few hypotheticals a week, you'll give them in a month the experience they would otherwise get in a year.

In general, coaching is useful for teaching your people to think better.

When you make a decision, always explain your reasoning. Not only because if you don't, people might guess the wrong reason, but also because if you do, you will teach your people to make better decisions.

Similarly, when you give feedback, always explain your reasoning. For example, if you say you like their work, explain what exactly you like about it and why. They will be more likely to do more of it.

Moreover, explaining your reasoning gives people the language and cognitive tools to explain their decisions to others.

Take the time to discuss things until they're crystal clear

Whether you achieve clarity *in your subordinate's mind* determines whether they will act effectively or not.

A superficial conversation that doesn't care about clarity, actionability, or readiness leads to superficial commitment and superficial action. Go beyond superficial.

Setting objectives during coaching

Every coaching session should end with the coachee having an actionable to-do list of actions they should take before the next session.

The keyword here is "actionable:" Once the session ends, they should be ready to spring into action. If they don't, it's probably because the tasks were unclear or too large.

I have found it helps to ask the coachee whether they feel ready to work on their to-do list or if they find any item unclear, daunting, or risky. Then, the coach and coachee can work together to make those tasks clearer, smaller, or less risky.

It also helps to be very specific and concrete while coaching, as opposed to generic and abstract. While you speak to your coachee, always ask yourself in the back of your mind, "What do I mean," and then voice your answer. Remember: the more concrete the objective, the higher its actionability and the lower the chances of misunderstanding.

A common question coaches have is, "To what extent should I set objectives for my coachee as opposed to letting him or her pick them?"

I believe you should have at least a say in the choice of the objectives. That said, you can try different approaches. It is important to notice what works and what doesn't. If you let your coachee pick their objectives, and that leads to satisfyingly fast progress, great! Keep doing it. If, instead, it doesn't work well, take a larger role in setting objectives.

When to coach

Ideally, coaching should become part of your weekly one-on-ones with your subordinates.

In addition to that, you might coach them during other one-on-one moments with them on an ad-hoc basis – for example, before an important meeting or presentation, e.g., mini-objectives to focus on while they present such as "don't make any *hmmm*" sounds or "improve your body language by always keeping your hands above your waist."

One-on-ones should last at least half an hour, even if there is nothing to discuss, *especially if there is nothing to discuss* **because there is always something to discuss.** If it looks like there is nothing to discuss, it means you should get better at asking questions or at handling silence.

The most useful pieces of information surface after a long, awkward silence: often, that's when the subordinate will voice what they were afraid to say – that's usually the most important piece of information.

Pro tip: one-on-ones are great moments to collect information about what's going on within your team. Ask questions such as, "What's the mood within the team?" or "Is anyone within the team experiencing any frustration?" This will be critical to inform your efforts to increase engagement.

Helping growth the via negativa way

(Via negativa refers to solving a problem by removing something old instead of adding something new.)

If you see some of your people spending a lot of effort yet making little progress forward, you might want to have a conversation with them about their beliefs about what brings growth.

There's nothing wrong with loving a part of their job so much that they're willing to go the extra mile even if it doesn't make a difference to everyone but themselves (I used to be like this with pixel-perfect Excel formatting). But it's problematic if those people are hungry for career growth and expect the energy they put into their work to reap some rewards. In this case, have a frank conversation with them and let them know that their effort and motivation won't matter if they don't direct them where it matters the most.

Of course, this conversation should be very tactful, and best if it doesn't look formal. You just want to come from a place of care and help them see something they might not be seeing.

Short- and long-term development

So far, we've talked about two forms of career development:

– **Long-term:** career paths.

– **Short-term:** development goals *(which, I remind you, aren't new positions or roles but skills and capabilities)*

The two are complementary, and you should use both. If you only provide career paths, only a fraction of your workforce will effectively take action on them, their progress will be slow, and you will leave a lot of effectiveness gains on the table. Conversely, if you only provide development goals, after some good results, your people's development and engagement will plateau, as they will start asking themselves, "What am I doing this for?"

Hence, use both. Ideally, **you want to talk about short-term development goals during almost all weekly one-on-ones, and review progress against career paths at a much lower frequency, just a few times a year.** That said, I advise you to talk about career paths at least every half year and possibly every quarter, providing feedback to your people on their progress and supporting them in growing faster, if they wish.

Summary

Instead of letting your employees in charge of their growth and them being disappointed when it doesn't happen (and the company losing out, both because its employees don't fulfill their productive potential and because they disengage), proactively stimulate them to grow.

To achieve this, you need both long-term career paths and short-term development goals.

Career paths should be available to everyone in the company, and there should be options for both vertical and within-position growth. They should be actionable documents that don't let their reader wonder, "I'm interested, but is this really for me, and what should I do next?"

Development goals should be specific, actionable, and achievable within a few hours of dedicated work at most. Managers should discuss them during each weekly one-on-one, stimulating personal growth and creating momentum in all of their subordinates.

In general, **understand that demotivation and disengagement are not inherent qualities of people but the result of having learned the lesson that efforts go to waste.** Therefore, find ways to direct the efforts of your people to tasks that will teach them the opposite lesson.

Give them outlets for growth. **Give them careers, not jobs.**

Politics

As a concluding note to this chapter, I noticed that **the more people are given constructive and actionable paths to growth and meaningful problems to work on, the less they engage in politics** – be it "party politics" or "internal company politics."

This is not a new effect – across history, decadence appeared downstream of the lack of serious problems.

The solution, though, is not to "create problems" or give meaningless objectives just for the sake of stimulation. Instead, the solution is to give meaningful objectives that stimulate growth and prevent complacency.

---

1. Do I really mean "everyone?" Not really. There will be a few employees who might have given up too long ago, perhaps even before joining your company, and have lost all trust that any improvement is possible. If they do meet their role's expectations but repeatedly fail to respond to stimulations, you might want to just accept that they won't grow and thus treat them accordingly. That said, this is a conclusion you can make only after having tried stimulating them as described in these pages, because for each such people who permanently lost all interest to grow, there are several who appear to have lost all interest but would respond to appropriate stimulation.

3

NEED #3: IMPACT AND RECOGNITION

When discussing impact, I often hear the following anecdote. Once, US President John Kennedy visited the NASA and asked a janitor what his job was. The janitor replied, "I'm helping put a man on the moon."

I don't know if the exchange truly took place, but the story spread and contributed to **the false belief that workers find purpose in the company mission.**

They seldom do.[1]

Instead, **people find purpose in seeing the difference their actions *directly* make to others.**

If you want to motivate a janitor, don't tell them they help send rockets to space. Instead, tell them that you really appreciate that, thanks to them, you get to use cleaner toilets at work than at your own house.

Inspiring mission statements are useful to get funding and media coverage but don't do much towards motivating employees – especially not those who don't work directly on the product or service.

Instead, most employees get the feeling of making an impact from two sources:

1) external customers (those who purchase the company's products or services), and

2) internal customers (the colleagues who are *directly* impacted by the employee's work).

Impact on external customers

Some ways to make your employees feel like they're making a difference for external customers include:

– Have your employees talk to customers or visit retail locations, especially during product launches.

– Record a customer telling their story and how the company's product or service impacted their life for the best, then share the recording within your team or organization.

Impact on internal customers

All your employees have internal customers: other employees who are positively affected if they do their work well and negatively affected if they do their work poorly.

You should make sure that your people see the impact they make on *their* internal customers.

Here is what does NOT work:

– Corporate-wide statements. Sending all employees a video collecting testimonials from selected employees doesn't work – most people watching that video don't really interact with those within.

– Anonymous statements, such as "your work impacts our retail staff." Who is this "retail staff?" Do they have a name? Do the people who receive that statement know them? If not, it won't count.

– **Generic statements,** such as "I appreciate your work." Generic equals superficial. It won't make an impact.

Instead, I've seen two things work: sincere, individual, specific thank yous from one's direct manager, and specific thank yous from internal customers.

Let's see how to do each.

Sincere thank yous from managers

Remind your people of the impact their good work makes.

Above all, avoid doing it in a way that sounds fake. Don't use corporate-speak, don't address your whole team at once, and don't use generic statements such as "I appreciate your work."

Instead, talk to your subordinates individually, pick a specific task or contribution of theirs, and tell them the concrete outcome of them doing their work well. For example, "Thank you for always sending those reports on time; you really help the finance folks get back to their families on time." Or "Thank you for the slides you prepared for John. I really liked how clean and engaging they were; they helped make the presentation memorable."

Don't overlook the mundane! In fact, **the more mundane a task, the more likely your employees** *feel* **it doesn't make an impact, whereas it probably does** - otherwise, why have them work on it?

The best approach is to look at your employees' typical workweek and ask yourself, "Which of their tasks are they most likely to think is worthless?" Then, remind them why doing that task well matters.

Avoid scheduling these "thank yous" in your calendar as regular occurrences. The more they become a chore, the less sincere you will sound. Instead, get into the habit of keeping an eye on what your people spend time doing, and every now and then, remind them of their impact.

Sincere thank yous from internal customers

My former manager used to invite internal customers to our office area to let us know what they needed from us, why, and the difference it made for them if we did our work well.

For example, I remember thinking that having to ask our potential clients to fill out a bunch of forms even before they signed a contract was a useless chore. Then, one day, Rachel from Finance came to our office and explained what happened to her if we forgot to ask the customer to fill out those forms: she would have to work overtime to correct the problem, and the company would be exposed to some risk in the meantime. Suddenly, my teammates and I understood the importance of that "useless chore." While it still felt tedious, it didn't feel frustrating anymore: we knew we were making Rachel's life easier.

I suggest you do something similar. Make a list of your subordinates' internal customers and circle the ones your team is less familiar with. Then, ask them to explain what they need from your team, why, and how they benefit from your team doing their work well. You can invite them to your team's workstations or have them record a short video. Either way, it will make a world of difference.

Recognition

In addition to knowing that they make an impact, your people also want to feel their work and problems recognized.

To recognize their good work, you can apply the advice you just read about communicating impact, with a key difference. **People only need to be shown signs of impact a few times per year, but they need much more frequently to know that their manager is noticing their good work.**

To understand why, imagine your manager asks you to prepare a report by Thursday. You spend a few hours working on it, and on

Wednesday evening, you send it. If you don't receive a thank you by Thursday, on Friday, you will start wondering if your manager cared about the report and whether you wasted your efforts working on it.

Hence, as a manager, you should always thank your subordinates for having completed the tasks you delegated to them – and you should do so without waiting too long, to avoid them doubting that their efforts went to waste.

Of course, if they completed the task unsatisfactorily, you should let them know, too. But never let them doubt you didn't care.

Moreover, always let your subordinates know you noticed any improvement (or lack thereof) they made on the feedback you gave them.

Again, never let any good work or improvement go unnoticed.

Acknowledge problems

I've conducted hundreds of interviews of workers, and this is the comment that surprised me the most for how frequent it was: "I would like my boss to see how difficult my job is."

In addition to being recognized for their good work, your people want the difficulties of their job to be acknowledged.

Is their job complex, exhausting, or difficult? They want you to notice.

You have two ways of doing this:

1) **Shadowing.** Spend 20 to 120 minutes watching them do their job. Then, acknowledge the difficulties they encountered.

2) **Talk about their work.** Ask them what difficulties they encounter, then listen. For some difficulties, you can and should help. Others are just part of the job. The most important thing is to make them feel heard.

Bring significance

People want their work to be meaningful to them and want to be meaningful to others.

They want their work to be significant.

However, you cannot make them feel significant with fake words. Or, more precisely, you can get away with doing that for the first few weeks until they notice that your words are empty and unsubstantiated by reality.

Instead, the question you should focus on is, "How can I create the conditions for my people to be significant?"

Explain what their work is about, help them figure out what their work *could* be about, support their growth, help them grow, create the conditions for them to grow, acknowledge their contribution, teach others to acknowledge each other's contribution, create the conditions in which people can do good work and be acknowledged for it, treat your people as individuals, teach your people to treat each other as individuals, create the conditions in which people can be treated as individuals, minimize unnecessary and meaningless job, create the conditions in which your people can spend more time on meaningful work, make it as easy as possible to be significant.

Constantly ask yourself how you can make it possible for your people to be significant.

Summary

Impact and recognition are about genuineness and connection.

Generic statements don't work.

Instead, **managers must take the time to connect the specific tasks their subordinates spend their time on with the specific people that those tasks impact.**

Doing so takes time but is also energizing and brings an enormous payoff both in terms of higher productivity and lower turnover.

Three initiatives are recommended:

– Collect high-quality video testimonials and stories from customers (external and internal) and show them to your people. Or, better, make it happen live.

– Give frequent reminders to your people of the impact of the *specific* tasks they work on.

– Take the time to shadow your people to let them know you are aware of the difficulties of their job.

---

1. In most cases, "the mission" isn't the cause of inspiration but just a confabulation. For example, most hospital workers aren't motivated by the mission, they're motivated by the fact that their work saves lives. The fact that the latter coincides with the mission is a mere coincidence.

4

NEED #4: BEING TREATED AS AN INDIVIDUAL

No one wants to feel like a robot or a cog in a machine.

The good news is that the solution is easy and inexpensive: treat your people as individuals.

The bad news is that you cannot do that with large-scale initiatives that group employees in an anonymous crowd. Nor can you do it with automated systems, such as birthday emails.

Instead, treating employees as individuals means to:

– Demonstrate a genuine desire to know what makes them unique. This could mean asking questions about who they are outside of work *(How do they spend their weekends? Do they have a family?)*, but it could also mean learning what makes them unique as an employee *(What do they care about? What are they uniquely good at?)*.

– Listen to them when they have ideas, complaints, or concerns. Do it *in person or over video calls rather than surveys or suggestion boxes.*

– Demonstrate a genuine concern for their well-being, for example, noticing when they're stressed or exhausted, or asking them if there's anything you can do for them.

Obviously, treating your employees as individuals could go too far, and it shouldn't. You want to ask them about their weekend a couple of times a month, not spend half an hour chatting every day. That said, that question should be genuine, and you should give your full attention to their answer (provided it's short; if the conversation drags on, feel free to politely cut it short after a minute or two).

Another way in which treating your employees as individuals could go too far is to listen to every concern or complaint of theirs, even unjustified ones, over and over. Instead, you should listen to every concern or complaint, but once you have a fair certainty that the concern or complaint is unjustified, rephrase your understanding of the situation and – if validated – explain empathetically yet firmly your opinion. It's particularly important that you explain your reasoning well, not just to prevent further similar situations but also not to appear arbitrary.

Respect

One component of treating your people with respect is to treat them nicely, critique the action, not the person, and generally be respectful.

Another component is, when they do something differently from what you would have done, to talk to them not with an attitude of, "You're wrong, and I'm right," but – at least first – with an attitude of, "I see you did X, why is that?" In other words, probe first whether they had a good reason to do what they did.

Employees treating each other as individuals

Ideally, you also want your subordinates to treat their colleagues as individuals, practicing the points above.

In some groups, this happens automatically: colleagues care about each other and spend a bit of time chatting or exchanging advice.

In other groups, this doesn't happen automatically, and you should do something. However, don't force anything at the group level, such as a "get to know each other" sessions: with the exceptions of onboardings, these sessions don't sound genuine. Instead, you can do three things:

– **Off-work hangouts.** These can work well, but make sure they're not too frequent or include excessive drinking or too-extroverted activities; otherwise, some colleagues might feel left out (in particular, the more introverted ones or those with a family). One meal or drink after work every four to six months generally works great.

– **Lunch breaks.** These are great opportunities to get to know each other during work hours without decreasing productive time. If you can, encourage your people to eat their lunch in a communal space rather than everyone on their own. As a manager, make sure you participate too.

– **Friday morning coffees.** I know of a few offices where employees are invited to have a coffee together in the communal room at the beginning of each Friday (or of the first Friday of the month). This is a great opportunity for employees to know each other, especially across departments. Clarify it's a time-limited event – you want your people to spend 15-30 minutes there, not the whole morning. Also, ensure that your local leadership participates, so that employees get to know their leaders and the other way around. Remember: people won't trust you unless they know you know them and their problems. Make sure that everyone can join the conversation, for example, by standing in an open circle and/or inviting people to have a coffee nearby.

If your team works fully remotely, you can recreate Friday morning coffees as virtual sessions; also consider yearly in-person meetups.

Summary

Your people need to feel like they are treated as individuals at work.

They don't expect this from the company – after all, it's not a person – but they expect it from their leaders.

And there's no shortcut to treating people as individuals other than to listen to them and interact with them in small groups or one-on-one.

Yet, it doesn't have to take much time. It just takes learning one's name and a couple of facts associated with them to transform a person from a robot into a human being. And it just takes listening to them once, thoroughly, to make them feel like they belong.

But it cannot be faked or done easily as scale. It requires a genuine connection.

5

NEED #5: REMOVING TOIL

People don't want to do unnecessary work or work on unnecessarily tedious tasks. They don't want *toil*.

Yet, many jobs contain plenty of toil, such as:

– **Unnecessary work** due to unclear delegation or poor planning.

– **Unnecessarily tedious tasks** that could be simpler or automated.

– **Being asked for information that doesn't get used,** such as reports no one reads.

– **Having to do additional work because of someone else's mistake.**

– **Unnecessarily long or purposeless meetings.**

– **Projects that get canceled.**

This chapter will help you make your subordinates' jobs as toil-free as reasonably possible.

The problem with toil

There are three problems associated with toil:

- **It's tiring, frustrating, and demotivating.** It also demonstrates a lack of care and respect towards the employees' time.

- **It takes time and energy away** from doing what makes the job interesting (such as creating impact or working on one's growth).

- **It creates work that doesn't add value,** which means work that cannot be rewarded, whereas we've seen in the introduction that the core principle of retaining talent is to create work that can be rewarded.

Hence, if you want to keep your employees engaged, you need to systematically remove sources of toil.

Let's see how to do this.

Removing toil from unclear delegation or poor planning

It's frustrating to work on something that gets canceled or reworked because delegation was unclear or planning was poor.

Here are four quick tips to improve delegation and planning.

1) Ask your delegees to rephrase. After you delegate a task, ask your delegee, "Just to make sure I didn't forget anything, could you please repeat your understanding of the task?" This simple question might surface misunderstandings or missing information that are easy to fix now but might involve lots of frustration, defensiveness, and blame to fix later on. Just make sure that you ask this question with the attitude of "wanting to make sure I have been clear" rather than "wanting to make sure you were listening."

2) Go into *concrete* detail. When planning or delegating, it's easy for everyone to understand what must be done on an abstract level, only for everyone to get back at their desk, start working on the project, and discover that they don't really have a good shared understanding of what must be done in practice. To prevent that, after having covered the project at a high level, go into concrete details. Ask the people involved, "Do you have any clear idea of what your next steps will be?" And don't just accept a yes, which people might say not to look bad, but also ask them what these next steps are. Don't do it with an attitude of testing them, though, but of care and wanting to help.

3) **Pre-mortems.** When a project ends, it's customary to hold a *post-mortem* meeting, where the project team reviews what went well and what went wrong, with the idea of extracting learnings for the future. Similarly, it's a good idea to hold *pre-mortem* sessions at the beginning of a project or task, where we ask ourselves, "Let's imagine that the project or task fails; what could have happened, and what can we do now to prevent it from happening?"

4) **Early check-ins.** When you delegate a task or project that takes days to complete, it's a good idea to schedule an early check-in a few days after delegation. This is a quick meeting for which you ask your delegee(s) to prepare an outline of what they will do and, if relevant, a sketch/sample/scheme of the deliverable. The idea here is not to evaluate their work but simply to catch any eventual misunderstanding or misalignment early on, before they spend too much time working in the wrong direction. The key is to adopt an attitude of "I respect your time and wouldn't want to have you spend any working in the wrong direction" rather than "I don't trust you."

I know some of the four tips above might feel uncomfortable, for no one wants to feel like a micromanager. But none of the tips above is micromanagement – they are just ways to pull forward in time discussions you would have taken place anyway. You want to have them before your people get frustrated by extra work due to a lack of clarity during delegating or poor planning.

Removing toil from unnecessarily tedious tasks

Some tasks are necessarily tedious, and doing them is one of the reasons workers are paid a salary. Other tasks are unnecessarily tedious, and doing them makes us wonder whether we are paid enough.

As a manager, you should review the tasks your subordinates spend time on, relentlessly remove any unnecessary parts, and simplify or automate the rest as much as reasonably possible.

One way you could do this is by sitting in your office and reviewing tasks and processes. This could be useful, but I would first recommend two other activities.

1) Shadowing. Spend ten to thirty minutes observing one of your people doing their work – as you would if you were a new hire on their first day. Clarify that this isn't to catch them wrong but to better understand their job and pain points. Take note of anything they do that could be automated, simplified, or not done at all. Then, check with your subordinate's internal customers whether your assumptions are correct. Finally, take action to remove toil.

2) Ask your people about toil in their work. This is done best during one-on-ones. Ask them questions such as, "Is there any task of yours which you feel takes longer than warranted?" and "Is there any task of yours which feels more complex or tedious than it should be?" Listen to their answers, but be critical of them. Sometimes, you will have to respond with "Sadly, this has to be this way, because of <good reason>," and other times with, "Wow, this indeed looks like it could be easier, let me see what I can do."

Here are two critical points on doing the previous actions right:

– **Don't make promises you cannot keep.** Better say, "Let me see what I can do," than commit to "I'll change this," only to later discover that there was a good reason why the task was done that way.

– **If you say you will "see what you can do," always follow up.** You should always go back to your subordinate with either "It's done, thank you again for your input" or "Sadly, I discovered it cannot be done because of <good reason>." If you instead forget about following up, the lessons you will teach are "my manager cannot be trusted" and "trying to improve processes is a waste of effort here."

Removing toil from interactions

Sometimes, toil emerges from interactions such as:

– **Having to ask for a piece of information over and over.** This might even lead to cultures where organizing a meeting is the only way to get people to give you the information you need, causing a vicious circle where people spend all their time in meetings and, therefore, don't have the time to share information in more efficient ways, such as emails.

– **Delegating tasks to colleagues and their output requiring massive re-work.** The root issue is likely either a lack of clarity in the delegation (in which case, use the delegation tips from earlier in this chapter), a lack of skills in the delegees (in which case, train and coach appropriately), misaligned incentives (in which case, get the appropriate managers in a room and solve the issue), or lack of time or staff (in which case, consider the costs of being understaffed in terms of lower quality, more difficult and costly talent retention, lower capability to absorb spikes in workload, and other problems).

You want to keep an eye on interactions within your team, and especially the mood thereof. Do people look energized or drained when interacting with each other or with other departments? If they look drained, what causes it? Is it something you can fix?

Removing toil from before & after work

For most companies, employees start working when they enter the company's premises. However, for most workers, work begins and ends with their commute.

If their commute creates toil or frustration, they will associate it with their work. Therefore, you should consider whether you can make their commute easier. A few possibilities include:

- Allowing hybrid or remote work.
- Having ample employee parking or bus shuttles.
- Allowing flexible work times, to allow avoiding rush hour.

Similarly, it's frustrating to work outside of work hours (e.g., answering emails). Find ways to keep this to a reasonable minimum. For example, teach your people not to send emails off-hours unless necessary (and otherwise use the "schedule send" feature in most email clients). Instead, policies such as "you don't have to reply to non-urgent emails" don't really work because many workers might reply anyway out of a sense of responsibility only to later feel frustrated for having felt the need to do so. On the one hand, you might feel it was their choice to reply to the emails; but on the other hand, you should acknowledge that, their choice or not, it is frustrating, and take action to prevent them from being put on the spot.

Systematically removing toil

In manufacturing, there is a concept called "Zero Defects."

It is an *aspirational* goal that consists of following each manufacturing defect with an incident investigation, in which the root cause is identified, a solution devised, and an action taken to prevent further occurrences.

Similarly, I advise your organization to adopt a Zero Toil attitude and follow each moment of frustration and each piece of unnecessary work with an incident investigation, root cause analysis, and preventive action.

Note that both Zero Defects and Zero Toil are *aspirational* goals that are *not* meant to be achieved. This is because getting to zero would mean not only addressing those problems that are worth solving but also those that cost a lot to solve compared to the benefits. Instead, these aspirational goals are about adopting an attitude of constant improvement. They are about saying, "Toil is not welcome here," "If you see toil, raise a hand," and "Let's design for toil minimization."

Overtime

While *some* overtime is a normal part of doing business, *chronic* overtime is a sign of poor organization and a source of toil for your employees.

Take the necessary steps (planning, staffing, demand smoothing, etc.) to ensure that your people don't do overtime that could have been prevented. Even if they don't seem to mind – they don't seem to mind *now*, but it "fills the vase before the proverbial last drop."

Toil from lack of skills

Sometimes, a task takes longer than warranted or is excessively frustrating because of a lack of skills. For example, it took me years to realize that I felt house chores were tedious because I didn't know how to do them properly, using tools and techniques that would allow me to finish fast.

Therefore, it's essential that you keep an eye open for skill gaps within your team and help them cover them.

The more skilled your people are, the less frustrating their tasks will be, and thus the more engaged they will be.

Frustration from unfairness

Another common source of frustration, especially between high performers, is seeing their colleagues operating at lower operational standards than themselves. As a manager, you have two options:

1) Clarify that everyone should operate at a high standard, praise those who do, and work closely with those who don't to bring them up to it.

2) Set a minimum standard and hold everyone to it; moreover, give those who operate at a higher standard a higher status, such as "seniors" or "experts."

I prefer #1 above, but as long as it's done consistently, #2 could also work; what doesn't work is the unfairness deriving from different standards being treated as if they were equal.

Ask your people

Ask your people how the processes and products they work on could be improved. You will get plenty of insights.

But there's a catch: you need to improve their job at least as much as you want them to improve your products and processes.

It's a question of mutual respect and trust.

You won't get much more of what you give.

Summary

Not only toil lowers your people's productivity, but it also destroys their engagement. Hence, you should proactively minimize it.

You might be tempted to implement top-down solutions. Don't forget about bottom-up ones, such as talking to your people or observing their work to understand their problems and perspectives.

Further readings

You might be interested in my books "Managing Remote Teams" and "Best Practices for Operational Excellence."

They are available on **Luca-Dellanna.com/books**

6

SUMMARY OF PART I

Before a summary of what we have seen so far, a quick question.

Have you ever noticed that, for many people, video games are more engaging than work?

This is because, in videogames:

– objectives are clear and concrete

– the player has full control (within boundaries, of course)

– feedback is immediate

– player progress is visible to them & frequently updated

– the roadmap and next step are clear

No wonder jobs that don't fulfill these characteristics aren't very engaging.

That said, don't get me wrong. This is not an advocacy for gamifying work, which is almost assured to backfire. Instead, it's an encouragement to read the list above again and ask yourself, "Is there any way I can bring these characteristics into my subordinates' work?"

Summary: the five needs

In the first part of this book, we have seen the five needs of employees to remain engaged.

Need	Examples
I want to earn a fair living	– I want to earn enough to satisfy my living standards – If I go above and beyond, I want to be compensated for it – I don't want others in the same role as me to earn more with no good reason
I want growth (and be helped to grow)	– I want my job and salary to evolve over time – I want to be supported in my growth (*i.e., the opportunities need not only to be there but I should be reasonably helped achieve them, e.g., through coaching and/or clear and actionable objectives for the next step*)
I want impact and recognition	– I want my manager to acknowledge the difficulties of my job – I want my manager to acknowledge when I do a good job – I want to see the impact I make with my work on its *direct*beneficiaries (customers, users, or colleagues)
I want to be treated as an individual	– I want my manager and colleagues to know a few things about me – I want my job to be adapted to my strength and weaknesses, within reason
I don't want toil	– I don't want my tasks to be unnecessarily tedious or tiring – I don't want to have to do extra work because of others' incompetence or lack of care

The five needs.

We have also seen a few ways you can help fulfill these needs:

1) **Compensation:** strive to pay market rates; pay fairly and consistently; explain why you think pay is fair; have consistent systems to align compensation across your organization; provide bonuses and raises as appropriate when your employees over-deliver; and stimulate individual growth to increase productivity *(see the next point)* to achieve the profitability required to pay higher wages.

2) **Growth:** provide everyone with the know-how and opportunity needed to grow, even those who don't demand it; work one-on-one with everyone and give them actionable next steps and short-term development goals; have clear career paths for everyone, both describing how to grow in new positions and in the current one.

3) **Impact and recognition:** remind each of your workers how they specifically impact their direct customers, be they internal or external ones; put such customers in front of them and let them tell their stories; consistently and frequently acknowledge your people's good work with specific and individual words; every now and then, shadow them or talk about their work, to know and acknowledge their difficulties.

4) **Being treated as individuals:** demonstrate a genuine interest in what makes your people unique; truly listen to them when they have an idea, complaint, or concern; demonstrate a genuine concern for their well-being; provide opportunities to get to know each other.

5) **Removing toil:** pay attention to proper delegation and planning to remove unnecessary work and re-work; ask your people which tasks feel unnecessarily long or tedious; pay attention to interactions that are tedious or frustrating and take action to improve them; adopt a Zero Toil attitude.

The second part of this handbook will guide you to apply what you have learned so far to create change at scale through your organization.

Before we move on, one last thing. **Be especially proactive in applying the advice of this book with your superstar employees, even if they don't seem super-engaged.** That's because there might be issues brewing that they will suppress (because they're professional) until one day, out of the blue, they might come to your desk with a resignation letter.

Pre-mortem this moment. Regularly ask yourself, "Let's imagine that today, my most engaged subordinate gives me their resignation letter. Likely or unlikely, let's assume it just happened. What would be their motivation? What can I do today to address this?"

Bonus: 10 ways to kill motivation as a manager

1. Ask your people to do things, then do not check whether they did them.

2. Ask your people to do things more carefully, then punish them for being slower.

3. Do not explain your decisions. Let your team think you didn't have valid reasons.

4. When someone shows motivation, do not give them opportunities to put it to use. This will atrophy them.

5. When choosing goals, be conservative. This way, even if your people achieve them, there won't be enough windfall to reward them.

6. When someone does something good, wait a few days before acknowledging them. Make them wonder whether their efforts went to waste.

7. When someone notices a problem, make them work overtime to solve it, even if they aren't the one having caused it. This will teach them to keep their mouth shut next time.

8. When someone underperforms, do not let them know until the yearly performance review. Let them believe they're on track for a raise until it's too late.

9. When delegating a task, do not check in with them early. If they misunderstand something, let them spend effort in the wrong direction before letting them know.

10. When delegating a task, only reveal part of your requirements. Then, when they deliver on them, be disappointed because they didn't deliver on the rest of your requirements, the ones you didn't mention.

PART II
CREATING CHANGE

The first part of this handbook taught you how to improve employee engagement and retention within your team.

The second part will teach you how to get other managers to implement the principles you just learned.

7

ROLLING OUT CHANGE

In theory, you could design a perfect change initiative, communicate to each of your employees what they have to do, and they would execute it perfectly, with results showing up quickly.

In practice, such an approach is likely to fail, especially if you never attempted anything similar before.

This is primarily because of three problems:

– **Complex plans never work as intended:** you can't have perfect information at design time, things and people change, etc.

– **You think you know what must be done but have no real know-how yet.** You don't know how to best communicate your change initiative, what questions people have when you train them, etc.

– **Because you try to change too much at once, you don't have the bandwidth to spend enough time and effort to change the behavior of a large group of people.** Changing habits requires a critical mass of communication, coaching, reminders, and feedback. You can only provide those with the necessary frequency if you focus on one part of the organization at a time.

Rolling out a change initiative

Here is a better approach to rolling out a change initiative.

1) Try to implement the change within your team. Implement the principles of this book to improve the engagement of your subordinates. How to do this will be the object of the next chapter. Observe what's intuitive and what requires practice. Note the questions and doubts people have. This experience will help you pre-empt the issues that might arise when rolling out the change initiative.

2) Pick one manager or supervisor you have a good relationship with – ideally a peer or a subordinate – and try to get them to implement the principles of this book. How to do this will be the object of a later chapter. Again, doing this will provide you with invaluable experience and feedback, and you will learn useful information to later be more effective in coaching other managers and deploying your change initiative at scale.

3) Pick one department, business unit, or business location, and get their managers to implement the principles of this book. How to do this will be the object of a later chapter.

4) Standardize the process in step #3 above and apply it to the rest of your organization, but no more than a few departments / units / locations at a time. Resist the temptation to rush this step, and remember that you need a critical amount of bandwidth to create momentum during the first weeks.

Capillarity

Here is a crucial concept when it comes to creating change. To explain it, let me use a metaphor.

The heart pumps blood into arteries, the arteries divide into vessels, and vessels divide into capillaries. Why?

That's because blood cells can only exchange oxygen with tissue cells that are adjacent.

Similarly, managers can only reliably change the behavior of those adjacent to them: those they know and are known by, that they see on an everyday basis, and that they trust and are trusted by.

Whereas communication using tools that scale (such as corporate-wide emails) is a necessary part of change initiatives, it is by no means a sufficient one. **You also need to push change through capillary links. That means, from managers to their direct subordinates, without skipping steps.**

No one is such a clear and persuasive communicator that they can write emails and documents that lead their readers to perfectly implement their content. That's why you will need to coach the managers you work with, and they will need to coach their subordinates, and ask them to coach their own subordinates, and so on.

It requires a lot of work, but it also works a lot. Whereas the alternatives require less work but also work less.

8

CREATE CHANGE WITHIN YOUR TEAM

My best advice is not to try too hard at the beginning.

Instead of trying to do everything at once, go back to the first part of this handbook, pick one action item, and take immediate action on it. Only after you're done, pick another action item. Don't overwhelm yourself. Allow yourself the time to learn from the interactions with your people.

It's better to do one thing right than five ones wrong.

Especially because doing one thing right will build trust and engagement, whereas doing something wrong will destroy them.

Common mistakes

– **Doing too much too fast.** If you have never practiced what this book suggests and suddenly start having all these conversations, it won't feel genuine. Moreover, if you do a lot during the first week and then slow down during the second one to catch up on other tasks of yours, it will feel like "this was another of these good-intentions initiatives that fizzle out and result in nothing changed," which is demoralizing. Instead, during the first couple of weeks, focus on doing a little and observing a lot. Notice what frustrates your people, what needs they have, what opportunities are there, and so on. It won't feel like much action, but it will help you be more targeted and effective later on.

– **Using tools that scale.** Resist the temptation to make a survey instead of talking to your people. You will get much better information and more context through a conversation. Similarly, don't do everything in a group setting; also use one-on-ones, in which people are more open.

– **Not being specific.** It's impressive the difference that being specific makes. When you give someone a generic comment, such as "good job," they might think it's courtesy. But if you say something specific, such as "I love that you always show up on time, even when there are back-to-back meetings," people will know that you meant it. Similarly, generic questions such as "Any feedback?" often produce nothing but politically correct commentary. Instead, ask specific questions, such as "Any task related to project management that feels unnecessarily long?"

9

INVOLVE OTHER MANAGERS IN THE CHANGE INITIATIVE

After a few weeks or months of working with your subordinates, you will have become ready to start involving other managers in taking the actions that will improve talent engagement and retention within their teams.

Doing this will involve lots of coaching.

In particular, if you have never coached anyone, I suggest you start by involving a single manager. Doing so will teach you valuable lessons about what you need to do or say differently and about common misunderstandings or obstacles. Only after a few months of working with a single manager will you be ready to involve others in your change initiative.

It's particularly important to follow this staggered approach because if you try to work with a lot of managers before you learn how to do it, you might commit a few errors that will decrease the trust those managers have in you and in the change initiative.

What's too little, what's too much, and common mistakes

– **Doing too little:** not having weekly coaching sessions, not roleplaying or playing hypotheticals during these sessions, not asking them about their challenges or reservations in implementing your suggestions.

– **Doing too much:** putting too much on the manager's plate, thus overwhelming them, or over-pushing your suggestions without surfacing or addressing their concerns, coming up with a plan that's more complex than a very simple roadmap consisting of a very few stages (you don't even need one, though if you want to create one, go ahead, just don't consider it set in stone).

– **Common mistakes:** focusing too much on the right things to do and not enough on how to do them right. Again, roleplay and hypotheticals are your best tools to teach know-how and validate that the delegee is set for success.

10

CREATE LOCAL CHANGE

Depending on your seniority level, this step might mean creating change within a department / business unit / business location.

To achieve this, you need to do both of the following:

– **Supporting change at scale.** This includes creating training materials[1] and large-scale communication. You might also want to find ways to evaluate progress.

– **Supporting change through one-on-one coaching.** This is an essential yet often overlooked step. Remember the principle of capillarity I mentioned early on. There's no alternative to ensuring that your people take action and they do it in the right way (rather than some superficial "check the boxes") other than one-on-one coaching. Of course, you cannot directly coach everyone. But you can coach the top 5-10 people in the department / business unit / business location where the change initiative is taking place, and you can get them to coach their subordinates, and they can coach their subordinates, and so on.

Common mistakes

– **Abstract training materials** do not work. Instead, your training materials must be concrete. For example, don't tell people, "You will have to coach." Explain what it means to coach. Use frameworks such as "bad / good /great" or "what's too little, what's too much, and common mistakes."

– **Corporate-wide communication only works if followed by the local manager explaining to their subordinates what that broad communication means** *for them in concrete terms.* Set expectations that all managers are supposed to do that. Coach them on how to do it properly.

– **Coaching is not optional** if you want your change initiative to work everywhere – not just where you are lucky enough to have exceptionally talented and engaged managers.

– **Tracking progress is important, but don't rely on surveys and metrics.** Don't get me wrong: they can be useful tools. But they are for spotting anomalies, not for describing reality. To know what's really going on, you will need conversations. Five 30-minute video calls with five random employees can teach you more than a corporate-wide survey.

Preventing virtue signaling

Once change initiatives become large enough, there is a tendency for them to degenerate into virtue signaling. A common symptom is some managers overdoing some of the actions suggested in this book – for example, making a point of theatrically reminding their people every day of the impact of their good work.

This is bad because employees are very sensitive to whether their manager is genuine and can sniff performative nonsense from far away. Moreover, pointless virtue signaling takes time away from more important uses of the manager's energy and attention.

You can prevent virtue signaling and overdoing by:

1) **Using the "what's too little, what's too much, and common mistakes" delegation framework** (in particular, making concrete examples of overdoing and virtue signaling in the "what's too much" part).

2) **Keeping an eye out for virtue signaling and privately telling them they're overdoing it.**

3) **Setting the expectation that everyone is supposed to give private feedback to each other whenever they feel that some action is performative or superficial.**

In particular, action point #1 above is critical and almost necessary, for it prevents problems instead of reactively addressing them and provides the groundwork for points #2 and #3.

---

1. If you are interested in training materials of mine, or other help, please email me: **Luca at Luca-Dellanna.com**

11

DEPLOYING CHANGE WITHIN THE WHOLE ORGANIZATION

I'll be blunt: for this to succeed, the CEO has to be fully on board.

This doesn't mean that you cannot do anything if your CEO isn't on board. Instead, it means that your ability to reliably create change is confined to the areas of the organizations whose leader is on board. For example, if you have a business unit leader or a country leader on board, great! Work with them first and create change downstream of them. The positive effects will hopefully help get your CEO on board.

That said, let's imagine your CEO is on board. You will basically have to repeat the playbook from changing a department or business unit but applied to the rest of the organization. This includes you coaching the CEO.

This might seem awkward, but remember: even the best hairdresser in the world requires someone to cut their hair, and the same applies to CEOs: having a coach helps even if the coach is less senior.

Of course, you won't coach them on being a CEO. Instead, you will coach them on deploying the change initiative and coaching their own subordinates (and requiring them to coach their own subordinates, etc.).

I could write a book on deploying change within an organization, but it would be distracting. The one thing that matters the most is good coaching, all the way from the top to the bottom. Moreover,

– **Good coaching takes place on a weekly basis.** Yes, there are exceptions, but you will be better off assuming that there shouldn't be any. The benefits of setting a few short-term action items and getting early feedback on eventual problems or obstacles are just too big to ignore.

– **Good coaching is one-on-one.** Yes, you can have group sessions, but this works better as one-off sessions before an important event (e.g., a launch) rather than as a long-term strategy.

– **Good coaching focuses on actionability.** It proactively probes whether the coachee is ready and committed to taking the actions discussed during the coaching sessions.

– **Good coaching doesn't only focus on what to do but also on how to do it well.** For this, roleplaying and hypotheticals are great tools.

– **Don't rely on formal systems and processes;** they are necessary, but they don't work well unless supported by their informal counterparts; i.e., you need to coach and manage your people so that they do things right even when there isn't a formal system and even for hedge cases.

Proceed step by step

All the above notwithstanding, I would still advise you not to attempt to change the organization at once. Instead, focus on one behavior at a time, one department / business unit / country / location at a time.

Take the time to build trust and set a consistent example.

You have limited time and bandwidth to do the required coaching. Don't spread yourself too thin. Only start the change you can support well.

In the long term, this will produce faster results.

Moreover, gaining good results in one area of your business will help bring people in other areas on board. By proceeding step-by-step, you will acquire know-how that will make the next steps easier.

Overcommunicate it

Don't just communicate your change initiative; overcommunicate it.

That's because **you only communicated something when it felt like you overcommunicated it.** Unless you repeat yourself, people will think what you said last week was last week's priority but isn't important anymore.

Hence, don't feel bad repeating yourself; it is worth it.

That said, managers are smart people who do not want to question the intelligence of their subordinates by repeating. Therefore, to avoid politeness getting in the way of effectiveness, you should make explicit the expectation that managers must overcommunicate.

Chapter summary

You might put a little bit of work into creating change every month for the rest of your career and achieve no change. Or you can focus your efforts for a few weeks and create sustainable change.

Proceed step by step and only as fast as you can while doing things well and achieving local critical mass.

Don't plan a strict timeline at the beginning of the project. Objectives are nice, but don't let them make you go faster than you can, with the result of creating no change at all.

CONCLUSIONS

In the first part of this book, we've seen the five needs of employees to remain engaged and how to fulfill them:

1) **Compensation:** strive to pay market rates; pay fairly and consistently, and explain why you think pay is fair; have consistent systems to align compensation across your organization; provide bonuses and raises as appropriate when your employees over-deliver; and stimulate individual growth to increase productivity and gain the profits required to pay higher wages.

2) **Growth:** provide everyone with the know-how and opportunity needed to grow, even those who don't demand it; work one-on-one with everyone and give them actionable next steps and short-term development goals; have clear career paths for everyone, both describing how to grow in new positions and in the current one.

3) **Impact and recognition:** remind each of your workers how they specifically impact their direct customers, be they internal or external ones; put such customers in front of them and let them tell their

stories; consistently and frequently acknowledge your people's good work with specific and individual words; every now and then, shadow them or talk about their work, so as to know and acknowledge their difficulties.

4) Being treated as individuals: demonstrate a genuine interest in what makes your people unique; truly listen to them when they have an idea, complaint, or concern; demonstrate a genuine concern for their well-being; provide opportunities for them to get to know each other.

5) Removing toil: pay attention to proper delegation and planning to remove unnecessary work and re-work; ask your people which tasks feel unnecessarily long or tedious; pay attention to involving people who are tedious or frustrating and take action to improve them; adopt a Zero Toil attitude.

Then, in the second part of this handbook, we've seen how to improve engagement across your company:

1) Proceed gradually. Acknowledge that there's a lot you don't know yet. So, start working to improve engagement within your direct subordinates; only then, start coaching another manager to improve engagement within their team; and only then, work with a larger scope.

2) Do things that do not scale. Do plenty of one-on-one coaching. Prefer a few one-on-one interviews to large-scale surveys. Insist that managers always explain to their team what organization-wide emails concretely mean for the team.

3) Coach, coach, coach. Don't just tell people what to do. Teach them also how to do it. Use roleplay and hypotheticals to give them feedback on how they do it. Set actionable short-term action points. Validate their readiness and commitment.

The path forward

I wish you all the best in implementing the principles of this book in your organization.

If you have any questions, please ask. You can email me at **Luca@Luca-Dellanna.com** – I read all emails personally and usually reply within 48 hours.

I can also help you with my coaching and consulting services. I have worked on organizational change initiatives for over ten years and have accumulated quite a lot of experience. I work both with individuals and companies. You can also read about my work on **Luca-Dellanna.com**

One last thing

I welcome feedback from all readers. In particular, I would love it if you sent me an email (**Luca@Luca-Dellanna.com**) letting me know:

– What, if anything, was unclear.

– Which unanswered questions, if any, do you have?

– What, if anything, could have been shorter or should have been longer?

Please share your learnings

If this book was useful to you, please share your learnings with others.

I would appreciate it if you left a review or talked about it on social media (feel free to tag me).

ABOUT THE AUTHOR
LUCA DELLANNA

An automotive engineer by training, after having led large teams and consulted for large multinationals, Luca quit his corporate job to become an independent researcher and author and dedicate his career to shedding light on the topic of emerging behavior.

After having lived in Spain, Germany, and Singapore, Luca recently moved back to his hometown of Turin (Italy). He spends his days between consulting, teaching, and conducting his research from his home, a coffee bar, or a park.

A few days a month, Luca also consults corporations and individuals that want to improve their businesses. Once per year, he teaches a Risk Management module at Genoa University, and a few times a year, he holds private intensive courses for entrepreneurs, operations managers, plant managers, and CEOs / COOs.

Luca writes regularly on Twitter (**@DellAnnaLuca**). You can visit his professional website and blog at **Luca-dellanna.com**. You can also contact him at **Luca@luca-dellanna.com** *(he reads all emails personally and usually replies within 48 hours).*

In the following few pages, you can read a brief overview of Luca's other books. You can support Luca by recommending this book to your friends or colleagues and leaving a review on Amazon.

    𝕏 x.com/DellAnnaLuca
    in linkedin.com/in/dellannaluca
    ▶ youtube.com/LucaDellannaChannel

ALSO BY LUCA DELLANNA

Winning Long-Term Games (2024)

Managing Hybrid and Remote Teams, 2nd ed. (2024)

Ergodicity: How Irreversible Outcomes Affect Long-term Performance in Work, Investing, Relationships, Sport, and Beyond, 3rd ed. (2023)

The Employee Engagement Handbook (2023)

The Pandemic Guidebook (2022)

100 Truths You Will Learn Too Late, 3rd ed. (2021)

Teams Are Adaptive Systems (2020)

The Control Heuristic, 2nd ed. (2020)

The Power of Adaptation (2018)

The World Through a Magnifying Glass (2018)

Winning Long-Term Games

The key to winning long-term games is to stop playing them as a succession of *separate* short-term games.

Yet, most people take the opposite approach. Here are three examples:

- The manager who sees each interaction with her team as a *separate* game. Every time she talks to her subordinates, it's to get things done rather than develop their skills. As a result, she fails to build the long-term assets (a competent team) she needs in order to win her long-term game (a successful career).

- The spouse who lies to avoid responsibility. If lying has, say, a 1% chance of being discovered, it is a great short-term tactic (it succeeds 99% of the time) but a terrible long-term strategy (if you lie once a week, you have a 99.5% chance of getting caught over a decade).

- The solopreneur who sends weekly emails to their mailing list and sees each as a *separate* game. They *consume* their audience's trust to generate more sales within a single email instead of *building* trust to create more sales within a few months.

These three examples show that approaching long-term games as a succession of *separate* short-term games is a bad strategy *despite working great over short time horizons.*

In "Winning Long-Term Games," Luca guides the reader into designing strategies that not only have a long-term horizon but also *leverage the long term* to gain an edge against anyone with shorter time horizons and make success all but inevitable.

Winning Long-Term Games is planned to be published in the first half of 2024.

Ergodicity: How Irreversible Outcomes Affect Long-term Performance in Work, Investing, Relationships, Sport, and Beyond (3rd ed.)

"This is one of the most important books I've read, period. It's short, articulate, and expansive on a singular subject matter — ergodicity, which is really the key ingredient to success in life, marriage, business, family, happiness, health, etc."

— *BLAKE JANOVER, JANOVER INC. CEO*

"A great book for those who quickly want to familiarize themselves with the concept of ergodicity. The author goes to great lengths to explain the concept in easily understandable terms. Highly recommended!"

—*AUKE HUNNEMAN*

Best Practices for Operational Excellence (3rd ed.)

"I'm a huge fan of High Output Management and Setting the Table [...] Luca's Best Practices for Operational Excellence took my management to the next level. It's been almost a month since I started implementing the principles, but I can already say that I've noticed a significant improvement in my company's morale [...] That feels amazing."

— *MOLSON HART, VIAHART CEO*

The Control Heuristic: The Nature of Human Behavior (2nd ed.)

"This book is like a magnificent suspension bridge, linking the science of the human brain to the practical craft of applying it in everyday life. I loved it."

— *RORY SUTHERLAND*

"A SUPERB book [...] by one of the profound thinkers in our field [behavioral economics]."

— *MICHAL G. BARTLETT*

"Luca's book was so helpful to my work. Opened my eyes up to some more reasons why change is so hard."

— *CHRIS MURMAN*

Managing Hybrid and Remote Teams (2nd ed.)

"Lots of specific and practical advice! Even experienced managers should find each chapter hugely valuable for reassessing their performance in each of the areas.

— *GABY LLOYD*

"Packed full of useful information. Luca takes the maddeningly difficult subject of managing a team and breaks it down into actionable activities. The sections on Clarity and Feedback are particularly strong, providing a way of viewing management as a nurturing and human activity.

— *DANIEL WEBB*

"Thought-provoking."

— *CARL BROWN*

100 Truths You Will Learn Too Late (3rd ed.)

"I am amazed at Luca Dellanna's ability to observe, compile, and articulate 99 very actionable life principles here. Each chapter describes the rule in a way that makes you think and then summarizes the Action. It's filled with DEEP insights yet VERY readable."

— *THERESIA TANZIL*

"Absolutely brilliant. You might have grasped some of these concepts before, but having them structured and in writing makes all the difference [...] I will surely recommend it to friends and co-workers."

—*ALBERTO PISANELLO*

"A very thoughtful piece of writing, deep and wiring!"

— *DAVID KREJCA*

The World Through a Magnifying Glass

"Thank you for helping me understand! My son was recently diagnosed, and I needed to be able to understand how he views the world. Why would certain things overwhelm him and cause so much anxiety and pain. This book made it so clear and easy to understand."

— *GEIGER T.*

Probably one of the best works I have read on autism (I have read a few), and it's surprising how realistically he depicts the condition."

— *MANEL VILAR*

"Loved The World Through a Magnifying Glass – this analogy NAILS IT."

— *EMERSON SPARTZ, NYT BESTSELLER AUTHOR*

ACKNOWLEDGMENTS

To my wife, Wenlin Tan, for the love and joy she brings to my life.

To my mother, for supporting and loving me all my life, and to Franco, for loving her. To my father, for the same and for stirring intellectual curiosity within me. To my family-in-law, for having raised my love and having accepted me as part of their family.

To my friends and everyone else who, directly or indirectly, knowingly or unknowingly, contributed to my well-being.

To my Patrons Scott Mitchell, Malcolm Ocean, and Pablo Cárdenas. Their help gave me stability on which I could conduct my research.

www.ingramcontent.com/pod-product-compliance
Lightning Source LLC
Chambersburg PA
CBHW070301220526
45465CB00004B/1699